MW01248614

DECODING STRATEGIES FOR EARLY READERS

DECODING STRATEGIES FOR EARLY READERS

Lucila Yolibeth Alcarese

Illustrated by Crystal Boudet
and Book Systems LLC

XULON PRESS

Xulon Press
555 Winderley Pl, Suite 225
Maitland, FL 32751
407.339.4217
www.xulonpress.com

Illustated by Crystal Boudet and
Book Systems LLC

Paperback ISBN-13: 978-1-66288-977-6
eBook ISBN-13: 978-1-66288-978-3

TABLE OF CONTENTS

INTRODUCTION

If you are a parent, paraprofessional, teacher or teaching intern, this is your guide to give children a foundation for reading success. In this book you will learn the fundamentals of phonics and decoding words. Phonics begins by teaching children to recognize letter and sound relationships which results in their ability to convert the written word to speech. This book will explain the 'how to' of phonics and decoding to ensure that persons teaching these skills and strategies will gain an in-depth understanding prior to instructing children. This book may challenge you, but you will be enriched as you gain knowledge to equip children with effective reading strategies that improve on pronunciation of words. English can be confusing. Why do some letters make different sounds? Why do different letters make the same sound? The English language has a rich and interesting history of incorporating words from other countries' languages, e.g French, Italian, Spanish, Russian and German... just to name a few.

In this book, you will gain knowledge of best practices', proven tips and tricks learned throughout my teaching career. Saxon Phonics is a type of curriculum taught in early childhood along with spelling that provides a crucial component in children's reading success. Teaching the foundational reading skills of phonics, phonemic awareness, and fluency is one of the most important goals of early childhood reading and reading intervention. Children will learn the spelling patterns within words. As you follow the step-by-step skills and strategies put together in this book, it will provide you with a solid path to reading success for a child. This was designed to help all children, including those with dyslexia, to receive support for on-going reading readiness and success.

Phonemic awareness is the ability to notice, think about, and work with individual sounds in spoken words. Before children learn to read print, they need to become aware of how the sounds in words work. They must understand that words are made up of speech sounds and phonemes. To become successful independent readers, children must acquire not only the basic decoding skills, but also reading fluency. Fluency is the ability for children to read expressively with speed and accuracy. Fluency is a necessary skill for developing reading comprehension. The overall goal is to teach children how to read through the foundation of decoding. This book provides helpful step-by-step decoding methods and phonic spelling strategies.

Having an understanding of the spelling patterns in words builds the foundation for strong readers. When kids and adults learn to read, they're connecting how these sounds are represented by letters. This book will provide you with the phonic spelling patterns rules to get your child ready to decode words, notice the patterns within the words, and targeted practice leading to successful reading ability. This book will guide those teaching these skills and strategies with step-by-step instruction for providing quality phonics instruction to younger and older children as well. Early intervention is the key to preventing struggling readers. This book is a proven step-by-step guide of how anyone can successfully teach a child to read or improve a child's current reading level. Learning common syllable patterns can help to become better readers and spellers.

To get started with your child we first need to understand the difference between a **vowel** and a **consonant**. The alphabet is made up of 26 letters, (5) which are vowels and the rest consonants. There are 21 consonants in the English alphabet. Although Y and W can sometimes count as vowels too. We cannot have a word without a vowel. To help your child remember here is a tip or trick for them to say: **vowels are: A, E, I, O, U, sometimes Y and W too when it's next to an O and it says O**.

The position of where "Y" and "W" are within a word will determine if it is a vowel or a consonant. If the "Y" or "W" are in the back of a word they are **vowels**. If the "Y" or"W" is in the front they are **consonants**. Vowels make many sounds. Not only must every word contain a vowel, but every syllable must contain a vowel sound. Vowels will either make a short sound, a long sound, or a schwa=/uh/. The schwa is the most common sound in the English language. Letter Y-changes its sound depending on where it is in a word.

THE ROLE OF Y IN WORDS

Y can be a consonant if it is in the beginning of a word. When you hear a /y/ at the beginning of a word spell it with a y.

Examples:	yellow	yes	young	yolk
	- the y is a consonant saying /y/			

Y=/short i/ usually make the short i sound when used in the middle of words.

Examples:	Symbol	gym	gypsy

"Y" AS A VOWEL - when it's in the back of a word it acts as a vowel. When you see a y at the end of a word, it won't sound like /y/.

The letter "y" can make the long /i/ sound at the end of the word if it is a one syllable word ending with "y" will say long /i/.

Examples:	Fly	sky	shy	why	dry
	by	sly	try	my	cry

The letter "y" in the back of the word can also say the long /e/ sound and acts as a vowel. If it is 2 or more syllable words ending with a "y" will say "e".

Examples:	family	Emily	party
	city	mommy	happy

Sometimes the y at the end of words has a vowel letter before it ay, ey, oy, uy-these words have patterns that will have their own vowel sound. ay (long /a/, ey (long /e/ or long /a/, uy (long i, oy (oy)).

day	key	they	buy	toy

The Vowels

A-E-I-O-U sometimes
Y and W too, when it's
next to an O and it
says "O"!

Vowels Open Syllable
"Long Macron"

 ȳ   fl ȳ

 ē ȳ   bā b ȳ

Y as a vowel- When it's in the back of a word it acts as a vowel. The letter can make the long I at the end of the word if it is a one syllable word ending with a "y" will say long i.

The letter y in the back of the word can also say the long e sound and acts as a vowel. If it is 2 or more syllable words ending with a "y" it will say "e".

WANTED

Y

For stealing the letters "E and I."

In 1 syllable words: Y sounds like "i"
shy, my, fly
Y sounds like "e"

In 2 syllable words: Family, Party, Early

$ $ REWARD $ $

WANTED "Y"

He steals the "E" sound
and the "I" sound

Teddy Tortoise

FLY MY SKY
FAMILY
PARTY EARLY

I'm wanted "Y". I can be sneaky in one syllable words, because "Y" can make the "I" sound. In two syllable words the "Y" can sound like "E". The "Y" steals the sound of "I" and "E". That is why he is wanted.

Decoding Clues

In one syllable words the "Y" sounds like "I" and in two syllable words the "Y" sounds like "E". Remember when "Y" follows a consonant it says "E" and sometimes "I". Only if the "Y" is at the end of a word. It is a vowel. Try saying the words on Teddy th Tortoise back. Remember this "Y" is wanted for changing th vowel sound.

In the box below vowels create a diphthong. Diphthong: a sound found by the combining of two vowels in a single syllable.

Since the Y sound for example (at the beginning of a word) is so distinctive and cannot be replaced by another letter. It is for this reason the letter Y is a consonant.

Y is a Vowel?

✓ When there is no other vowel in the word Y is usually a vowel, like the word gym.

✓ When the Y is after a consonant at the end of a word, like the word happy.

✓ When the Y is after a vowel at the end of a word, like in the word honey.

✓ When the Y is at the end of a syllable, like in the word loyal.

✓ When Y is in the middle of a syllable, like in system.

Y is a Consonant?

✓ When the Y is at the beginning of a word, like in the word yellow.

✓ When the Y is at the beginning of a syllable, like in canyon.

Decoding Clues

The vowel "Y" is a semi-vowel. This means that sometimes it is a vowel and sometimes it is a consonant. This also means that it creates a word called a diphthong. A diphthong is the sound found by combining two vowels in a single syllable.

Examples are:
OY, OI EW, OU, OO, OW, AU, AW

"W" can be a **consonant** when the w is at the **beginning** of a word. W can be a **diphthong. A diphthong** is a sound made when you see two vowels side by side, and it makes a distinct sound known as a **gliding vowel**. To make this sound remember this story: If you got stung by a bee you would say "ow"! Common used diphthongs in English are: oi, oy, ee, ea, ai, ay, ou, ow, au, aw, oo, ew, ue. If a diphthong doesn't sound right then you have a **vowel diphthong** when it's next to an "O" and it says O. A vowel diphthong is when you see a double vowel sound combination of 2 vowels next to each other that creates one sound. That means a vowel diphthong starts as one vowel, then moves to a second vowel. (2 vowels, 1 sound, same syllable)

Examples: (w as a consonant when the w is in the front of words)

| wax | wedding | wacky | water |
| win | wait | why | web |

OW can be a diphthong when it says "ow" as if you got stung by a bee you would say "ow"! The spelling patterns you see will be ou/ow words that make a distinct sound sometimes known as the gliding vowel. The difference between /ou/ and /ow/ is that /ou/ is found in the front and middle of a syllable word. /OW/ is found in the back of words. But be careful because /ow/ sometimes doesn't say /ow/ it can say /o/ where the /w/ might be silent.

When you hear /ow/ at the start of, or inside a word, use /ou/. /ow/ is found in the beginning, middle or end of words. The /ow/ sound is followed by an l or n usually spelled with ow, when it's alone at the end of a word. The ow sound is irregularly spelled with the ending of er or el will usually be spelled ow. When you hear /ow/ at the end of a word or syllable use ow.

cow	frown	how	brown	now
howl	crowd	clown	town	down
cloud	house	loud	vowel	mouth
mouse	flower	proud	ground	shout

A vowel dipthong acts as a vowel team (2 vowels next to each other) where the second sound is silent and the first vowel is long. But be careful because /ow/ sometimes doesn't say /ow/ it can say long /o/ where the /w/ might be silent and act as a vowel.

Example:	know	snow	grow	bow	slow
	show	row	blow	throw	pillow

Consonants in the English alphabet is a speech sound that is not a vowel (a,e,i,o,u). Consonants make only one sound and can be defined as speech sounds that obstruct airflow in our vocal tract. Both consonants and vowels are very important in order to pronounce almost every word in the English language. Without vowels or consonants, it would be impossible for us to communicate clearly. Consonants and vowels make speech clear and easier to understand.

"W" can be a consonant when the "W" is at the beginning of a word. It becomes a vowel or a diphthong when it's next to an "O" and says the vowel sound "O".

Decoding Clues

When can the letter "W" be used as a semi-vowel. Say the phrase below.

How now, brown cow.

All four words in this phrase make the /uu/ vowel sound and the "W" is at the end of each word. Put your lips together like you are going to blow a kiss and say the phrase again. It can be used in a

Vowel Team

(aw, ew, ow)

These vowel team are referred to as diphthongs. Words of the English origin in the English language don't end in the letter "U". In your spare time practice the words below with the *Vowel Teams*.

owl saw drew bow
lawn crowd crew

Words with "W" as a consonant.

Wax, Wacky, Water, When, Why, What, Where

Words that have "W" as a semi-vowel or diphthong.

Owl, Pow, Cow, Now

When the "W" makes the vowel sound.

long /$\overline{O}$/.

These words are below.

Know, Blow, Show, Glow

Decoding Key

v– Vowel

c - Consonant

v̆c - short breve

v̄ - long macron

v̄v̄ - vowel team

v̄v̄ - team villain

vv - EAT or EAD that can be long or short

v̄ce - vowel consonant e
         aka "bossy e"

ə– schwa, makes
   the "uh" sound

s̶ – z sound

ç - cedilla c sounds like an s

c - aka k back, turns the c into a k sound

ge - makes a j sound

i / e
y / y - can be e or i

ü - makes the oo sound

qu - q is always next to u

f
ph - sounds like an f

igh - gh are ghost letters that are silent

final stable syllable - has a consonant + le. Ex: apple

DECODING STRATEGIES

CVC words
Consonant Vowel Consonant

Spelling Pattern 1: **CVC** words stands for a "consonant, a vowel, and a consonant. A vowel followed by a consonant is short: Code it with a breve. A **breve** is a symbol (˘) written or printed above the vowel to show that is pronounced with a short sound. When a syllable ends in a consonant, the vowel makes its short sound. The pattern in the following examples are **CVC** short breve words. To make it simple, ask your child to find the vowel and look at the letter behind the vowel and ask if it is a vowel or a consonant? If it is a consonant the vowel will make a short sound. Code it with a short breve. (˘) **VC vowel consonant** the symbol goes above the vowel. This is a closed syllable which ends in at least one consonant; the vowel is short. Consonant sounds are made with part of the mouth touching or momentarily closed. This slows or stops the flow of air leaving the mouth. Most words contain consonant sounds.

Practice with these words to see the spelling patterns.

Sample of words:

cat	rug	at	cup	had	pop	cab	bat
nap	ran	map	hot	red	dog	pup	gas
ham	jet	met	yell	bed	vet	fan	kid
duck	van	pet	top	bug	nut	mud	van
men	lip	leg	nut	red	big	sit	egg
dad	cap	map	pig	fib	bag	hen	dig
lip	ten	rip	red	pet	fat	hit	gum

VOWELS AND CONSONANTS

Vowels and Consonants are sounds used to make words.

VOWELS

A E I O U

The letter "Y" is special.

Sometimes "Y" is a Consonant.

Sometimes "Y" is a Vowel.

Decoding Clues

When the "Y" is in the front of a word it is a consonant.

When the "Y" is in the back in a word it is a vowel.

The words below have vowels and consonant. Mark a V over the vowels and a C over the consonants.

AKE TIME GRADE FUN

PPLE LIME APE MONEY

CONSONANTS

B C D F G H J K L M
N P Q R S T V W X Y Z

Use the alphabets below to put vowels in the box under **Vowels** and letters in the box under Consonant box.

Vowels letters	Consonants letters

A B C D E F G H I
J K L M N O P Q R
S T U V W X Y Z

The words in this box have "Y" as a Consonant and "Y" as a Vowel. The words in **Red** have "Y" as a **Vowel** and the words in Blue have "Y" as a Consonant. Look at each word. Point at the "Y" in each word and say if it is in the front or the back.

Yellow **Gym** Yes **Happy** Young

Shortie Short

A vowel followed by a consonant is short. It is coded with a short breve symbol: ˘

SHORT VOWEL WORD LIST

ă

Short a words:
cat, bat, map, lap, rap, at

ĕ

Short e words:
bed, red, get, wet, jet, set

ĭ

Short i words:
big, pig, lit, fit, kid, lid

ŏ

Short o words:
got, hot, not, lot, pot

ŭ

Short u words:
cup, cut, hut, mud, rug

SHORT VOWEL WORDS

Decoding Clues

A Breve is a symbol above the short vowel to show that it is pronounced with a short sound. It is coded with a Breve: ˘ This means the vowel says it has a short sound.

Shorty Short has those words on his back. An open syllable ends with a vowel sound that is spelled with a single vowel

(a,e,i,o,u)

Decoding Clues

CVC: Consonant Vowel Consonant in these words the stress is on the vowel. The vowel sound comes after the Consonant like in the words on Sidney Short's back. Some other examples are on this page.

Sidney Short

Consonants

Bat
b

Cat
c

Mice
mice

Dinosaur
d

Music
musi c

Frog
f

Goat
g

Giraffe
giraffe

Horse
h

Consonants

Jellyfish
j

Kangaroo
k

Lion
l

Monkey
m

Nightingale
n

Drink
drink

Consonants

Turtle
t

Vulture
v

Wolf
w

Xingu River Ray
x

Yak
y

Zebra
Z

Vowel Closed Syllable

CVC Words

ă   ăpplĕ

ĕ   ĕlĕphănt

ĭ   ĭglōō

ŏ   ŏctŏpŭs

ŭ   ŭmbrĕllă

g- sounds like j
y - makes a short
i sound because
it's acting like a
vowel in the word.

ў   gym

LONG MACRON

SPELLING PATTERN 2: **Macron** - Derived from Ancient Greek it is a diacritical mark: it is a straight bar (‾) placed above a letter, usually a vowel. **Code it with a macron**

(‾) and an accent (´) . The **macron** correctly pronounces many foreign words that have relocated into the English language.

If a word ends in a vowel and there is nothing after the vowel, it will be coded with a long macron. This means the vowel would say its own name. The vowel is a loud sound saying its name. An open syllable ends in one vowel; the vowel is usually long. What happens to your mouth as you say these sounds?

/i/	/a/	/e/	/o/	/u/

Your mouth gradually opens wider. Vowel sounds can be stretched out. Every word must have a vowel sound. Practice with these examples below.

me	he	go	no	we	she	hi	so

Words that have a v/cv or v/ccv spelling patterns still follow this rule. When one consonant stands between two vowels we divide the syllables after the first vowel. In v/cv and v´/ccv words we make the first vowel long by stressing the syllable or raise our pitch to the first vowel and divide the word. Examples of words that follow this are: e/qual, pro'/gram, mu'/sic The same follows for a word that has an v'/ccv pattern. Practice with these patterns below.

equal	table	tiger	program	spider
music	bacon	broken	basic	silent
hotel	robot	baker	secret	taken

Kid Long

(-)

macron

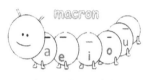

Long Word List

Long a words:
bay, cake, pay, baby, way

Long e words:
key, me, free, bee, tea

Long i words:
night, kite, site, light, lite

Long o words:
boat, goat, toad, road, snow

Long u words:
unicorn, useful, cute, unique, uniform

Decoding Clues

The mark above the long vowel is call a long macron and it looks like a line (-) above the vowel in words. Sometimes the first vowel does the talking and the second vowel does the walking. It is silent. The macron is on all the vowel you see on Kid Long's back.

An open accented vowel is long. It is coded with a macron: "-". This means the vowel says it has a long sound. The long macron is a line above the vowel.

Vowels Open Syllable
"Long Macron"

$\bar{a}$ cake
vcv

_+_= $\bar{e}$ $\bar{e}$quạl
vcv

$\bar{i}$ $\bar{i}$ce
vcv

"Cedilla c makes
the s sound."

$\bar{o}$ boat
v

$\bar{u}$ $\bar{u}$nicọrn
vcvc

Vowel teams or Vowel Digraphs

SPELLING PATTERN 3: **Vowel teams or vowel digraphs is a spelling pattern that uses two letters that unite to make one sound.**

Vowel Teams- Vowel teams are groups of letters that work together to make a vowel sound (usually a long vowel sound). When two vowels are side by side, sometimes the first one does the talking by having the long vowel sound and the second vowel is silent. Vowel digraphs combinations of two vowels that produce a single sound. In English, there are several vowel digraphs or combinations of two letters that represent a single sound. Sometimes w and y will function as a second vowel. The patterns in words you will notice are: aw, ay, ow, oy are some examples.

The letter 'y', 'w', 'gh' or 'r' are also used in representations of vowel sounds (as in 'ay', 'ow', 'igh' an 'er'). You will have a vowel pair syllables or vowel team when you see an (ai, au, aw, ay, ea, ee, ei, eu, ew, ey, ie, oa, oe, oi, oo, ou, ow, oy, ue, ui).

Sometimes two vowels work to form a new word. We have 18 vowel sounds in English, but only 5 vowel letters which represent them so it is necessary to use combinations of the vowel letters. When two vowels are side by side to represent one sound it's called a **'vowel digraph'**. The letters 'y', 'w', 'gh' and 'r' are also used in representations of vowel sounds (as in 'ay', 'ow', 'igh' and 'er'). Vowel team (ai, ea, ie, oa, ee, ay, oe)

Examples:

rain	each	bean	mean	pie	bow
tray	boat	sheep	bleed	play	cheese
feet	meat	seat	neat	plain	goat
queen	seed	bead	green	road	sea
coat	clean	bee	tea	team	weak
pain	boast	day	bow	train	peach
brain	lie	dream	soap	leaf	maid
wait	heat	pay	street	sheet	team

Vowel Teams Syllable

 au

 aw

ea eagle

ĕa head

ēa steak

ee feet

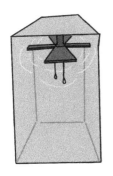

ēi̶ c̶e̶i̶ling

 ēi̶ ēi̶g̶h̶t̶

 eu e̶u̶ropē̶

 ew scrēw

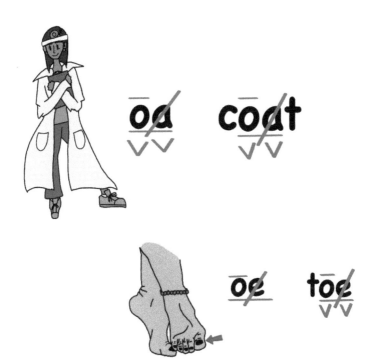

ōa cōat

ōe tōe

 oi coin

 oo   book

 oo   spoon

 ou   house

 ou   soup

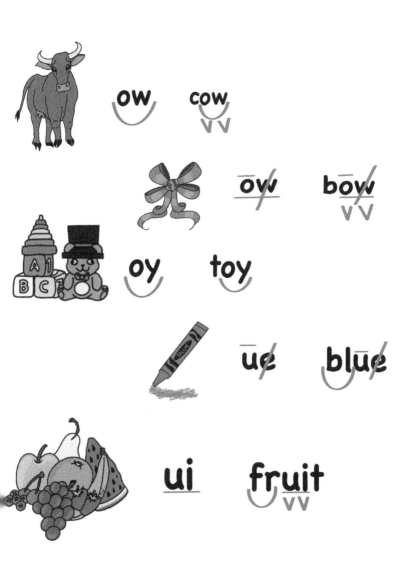

ow   cow

ow   bow

oy   toy

ue   blue

ui   fruit

There are some words in which the second vowel is the one that is pronounced. Sometimes I have taught them as the VOWEL VILLAINS who are unpredictable vowels. As with most rules in the English language there are exceptions. These exceptions are called "unpredictable vowel teams" or code overlap. Sometimes the phonic rule may break, that's why you have to test the word to see which vowel is speaking (usually a long vowel sound) either the first or the second vowel and the other vowel is silent. Have your child test the word to see which vowel is long and which is short when pronouncing the word.

Examples:

break	steak	niece	piece
believe	thief	yield	shield
grief	field	brief	great

YOU WILL NOTICE IN THE SPELLING PATTERN THE SECOND VOWEL DOES THE TALKING (USUALLY A LONG VOWEL SOUND) AND THE FIRST ONE IS SILENT.

Whenever you have the **EAT** pattern or the **EAD** the vowel may be LONG or SHORT. You can test out the word to see which one is pronounced correctly to form an actual word.

Examples of words with this pattern are:

feather	meat	bread	ahead	read or read	
dead	lead	spread	head	neat	leader
tread	great	wheat	cheat	seat	beat
treat	repeat	thread	spread	plead	instead

Vowel Teams: two or more letters that combine to represent a vowel sound. When two vowels are side by side, sometimes the first one does the talking and the second one does the walking. (Meaning it's silent) Vowel teams look like this:

(ai,ie,ea,ee,ay,oe.oa)

NOW YOU SHOULD NOTICE THAT THE **SECOND** VOWEL DOES THE WALKING AND THE **FIRST** VOWEL DOES THE TALKING. VOWEL TEAMS COULD ALSO HAVE A **DIPHTHONG**. THESE WORDS HAVE (OU, AND OW) EXAMPLES ARE UNDER THE **UNPREDICTABLE VOWEL TEAMS** BELOW. Sometimes the second vowel does the talking, when they act as **Vowel Villains**. Test these words under **Unpredictable Vowel Team** by sounding them out.

PREDICTABLE VOWEL TEAMS

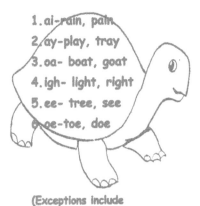

1. ai-rain, pain
2. ay-play, tray
3. oa- boat, goat
4. igh- light, right
5. ee- tree, see
6. oe-toe, doe

(Exceptions include Shoe and canoe)

UNPREDICTABLE VOWEL TEAMS

1. ea- break, steak
2. ie- piece, believe
3. oo- moon, book
Diphthongs:
4. ow- cow, snow
5. ou- loud, soup, out

(Diphthongs are made up of a combination of two vowels. They make a combined vowel sound. Like in toy and soil.)

Vowel Teams

Sometimes two vowels work together to form a new word.

Vowel Teams

See a blend	Blend it	Read it
aw	P-aw	Paw
au	V-au-lt	Vault
al	B-all	Ball

Long U Family

ew ue oo eu u_e

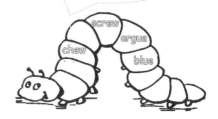

Digraph and Blends
Vowel Teams

chew		cue
drew		due
flew	**ew ue**	blue
grew		glue
screw		argue

Use the blends "EW" and "UE" mostly at the end of words like the ones on Elly inch worm.

Decoding Clues

Diphthongs is also a vowel pattern. These diphthongs are made up of two sounds. That means a diphthong starts as one vowel, then moves to the sound of the second vowel.

Examples of diphthongs are (oi, oy, ee, ea, ai, ay, ou, ow, au, aw, oo, ew, and ue)

In a diphthong two vowel make one sound. Like in the words out, now, and hay.

Decoding Clues

Vowel Teams is a spelling pattern that uses two or more letters to represent a single sound. The patterns look like (aw, au, ew, ue, ai) and more eve "oo"

A vowel team syllable is a syllable with a long, short, diphthong vowel sound that uses a letter combination fo spelling.

short vowel sounds

a: cap, bat, mat, lap, rap, tag, bag
e: bed, peg, get, wet, led, jet, net
i: rid, kid, rig, fit, pit, lip, big
o: got, not, mop, cog, hot, rod, pot
u: cup, hut, cut, pup, mud, rug, tug

These short vowel words have one syllable.

VCE- Vowel Consonant E Syllables

SPELLING PATTERN 4: **Vowel-consonant-e syllables end in one vowel, one consonant, and a final e. The final e is silent, and the vowel is long.**

This spelling pattern is a word that ends in a final silent e with a consonant just before the silent e. The silent e makes the vowel before a long sound. Code the vowel with a long macron, and cross out the silent e. Basically if a word has an E at the end it's a Bossy E aka Sneaky E. Bossy E is rude, he is a bully and makes the vowel scream its name by having the long vowel sound. **So the 1st vowel sounds like its alphabet name and the 2nd vowel is silent.**

Words that follow this pattern are:

ape	concrete	like	rope	tube	hope
name	robe	five	save	game	mute
tape	poke	bake	flame	page	kite
change	wage	place	cake	vote	nose
dime	hose	cute	cone	theme	grade
quite	prize	line	time	slide	hope
rude	huge	use	bone	shape	choke

BOSSY "E"

BOSSY "E" POEM

When Bossy "E" is at the end of a word. The first vowel has to say their name.

Bossy "E" is rude. He is a bully. He makes the first vowel scream its name. By having the long vowel sound.

Sound out the words below by putting a long macron (-) over the first vowel that does the talking.

Name, Like, Cake, Rope

Decoding Clues

When you see Bossy "E" at the end of a word the first vowel says their name and that bossy "E" is quiet.

Bossy "E" is silent and rude he makes the first vowel scream its name. By having the long vowel sound. So, the first vowel sounds like its alphabet name.

Here are some words that have a Bossy "E". Point out the words that make a vowel say their name.

(A, E, I. O, U)

back, Pete, Sam, bike, rose, cute

Mark an X through the words that don't have a Bossy "E"

cute

When "Y" is in a two-syllable word it says the vowel "E" sound. Like in the words below.

Baby, Money, Funny, Honey

Bossy "E" can sound like "E". Say the words on Inchy Sue's back.

five name these

Decoding Clues

Bossy "E" is quiet in a word he has the other vowel say their names. If you see the "E" at the end of the word. It rides at the end of words like the ones on the Anny the inch worm's back.

USE YOUR DECODING CLUES

time
hope
slide

Consistency improves Fluency and develops reading comprehension.

Learning how my vowels work makes me a better reader.

Vowel Consonant E Syllabl

aka "Bossy E/Sneaky E

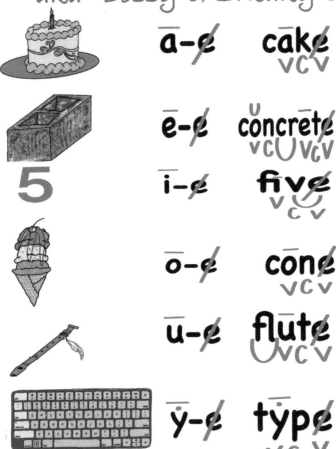

ā-ȩ cāke
vcv

ē-ȩ cŏncrēte
vcŭvcv

ī-ȩ five
vcv

ō-ȩ cōne
vcv

ū-ȩ flūte
ŭvcv

ȳ-ȩ tȳpe
vcv

Schwa=short /uh/

Code with an upside down e (ə schwa).
The Lazy Sound

SPELLING PATTERN 5: V/CV the vowel will be a schwa=short /uh/ sound. Code with an upside down e (ə schwa). A schwa is a vowel sound in an unstressed syllable, where a vowel does not make its long or short vowel sound. It usually sounds like the short /u/ sound, but softer or weaker. The schwa sound is a short vowel sound or a lazy vowel. The schwa is a muffled vowel sound that only appears in unstressed syllables. It is actually the most common sound in English.

A word that has a vowel, a consonant followed by another vowel spelling pattern you would divide the vowel away from the consonant and make it a schwa sound=short uh sound. Schwa is most simply defined as the sound a vowel makes in an unaccented syllable. A schwa can be spelled with any vowel. It is known as the lazy vowel. Teach your child to try the schwa sound if a word does not sound quite right with a short or long vowel pronunciation, try a ə schwa sound. Sometimes it makes a neutral sound /uh/ sound. It can appear at the beginning, middle or end of the word depending where the stress is. Unstressed words and syllables are usually said faster and at a lower volume than stressed words or syllables. Once we understand the schwa then we will become better at the correct pronunciation of a word. Each word has at least one vowel stress position and the rest of the word would be unstressed. A schwa is found in unaccented syllables. Practice with the example on the page.

Some spelling patterns of words that follow this example are:

above	a	woman	upon	physical
about	the	finally	international	across
alone	sofa	banana	of	away

If a word ends with an a at the end it also is a **schwa**. Find and Identify the a that says schwa short a.

banana	lava	mama	diva	yoga
diploma	camera	area	visa	data
dilemma	gorilla	idea	comma	umbrella
zebra	aroma	pizza	umbrella	sofa

Here are some spelling patterns to help you know when there is a schwa. If a word begins with an 'a' followed by a consonant it will have a schwa if the syllable is unstressed. When the vowel does not make its long or short sound. Usually it will sound like the short /u/ sound, but softer and weaker.

Examples:	across	along	around
	about	above	away

Also there are exceptions to the spelling pattern rules:

If a word begins with an 'a' and it is stressed then it will not have a schwa sound.

Examples:	able	actor	artist
	agreement		acre

LiL SCHWA

ə

SCHWA is the short vowel sound because it can be spelled with any vowel including "Y". Known as the lazy sound. SCHWA never "stresses". The symbol for SWCHA looks like an upside down "e".

ə

An example of this sound is in words below

bananá mamá thə

"Schwa"

pĕncĭl
VCCV

hŏspĭtăl
VC VCV

royăl

A vowel before the letter "I" or "L" at the end of the word is usually a SCHWA sound that makes the "uh" sound.

In British accent word endings such as er, ar, or, our or ure are pronounced with a schwa sound. R-controlled vowel combinations have an "r" coming right after a vowel. We have five control vowel word endings *ar, er, or, ir* and *ur*. Sometimes we call it "bossy r," because it makes the vowels change their sound. Words with Mr. Bossy R has a special sound. Vowels followed by r do not make their common short or long vowel sounds. When we have a word that has a vowel that is followed by r, the vowel is controlled by the r and makes a new sound.

Practice pronouncing these words that have the controlled r vowel combination.

teacher	her	learn	dollar	flower
dinosaur	different	summer	water	doctor
secretary	leader	purse	corn	star
shark	power	yarn	barn	shirt
butter	star	car	girl	bird
purple	turtle	other	sport	card

Compare the words on my back to your answers.

SURF
FERN GIRL

Decoding Clues

Bossy "R" is controlling the sound of the words. This is called a VOWEL DIGRAPH they are (er,ir,ar,or,and ur) On a blank sheet of paper add a Bossy controlling "R" to the words below to make the sound of the vowel digraph.

fe_n, bi_d, bu_n, he_b, gi_l, and su_f st_ and h_n

POEM

Controlling "R" is in the "ROAR" of a lion and the "SOAR" of a "BIRD". That little bossy "R" is even in grandpa's "SNORT".

WHEN YOU SAY THIS POEM MAKE THE CONTROLLING "R" SOUND LOUD.

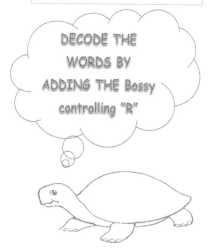

DECODE THE WORDS BY ADDING THE Bossy controlling "R"

BOSSY "R" WORD SORT FUN

AR	OR	ER/IR/UR

Bossy R likes to change the vowel that comes before it!

BOSSY R WORD SORT

Use the words below to fill in the word sort above. Look at each word and sound it out.

ART, CAR, STAR, FORK, STORM, CORN, ALERT, BIRD, TURN

RED, YELLOW, AND BLUE. DID COLORING THE WORDS HELP YOU?

Bossy "R" likes to be in charge. Be aware, that "R" changes the vowel in the words.

The reason I'm so bossy is you must sound out the vowels that are usually in front of me.

Words with the Bossy "R" make a special sound.

Sound out these examples:

AR! OR! ER/IR/UR

Vowel-R Syllables
R-controlled vowel combinations

 ar star ar dollar

 er flower

 ir bird

 or corn or doctor

 or worm

 ur purple

Final Stable Syllables Consonant -le

A final stable syllable is a word that has a syllable that is at the end of a word that makes a unique sound. Many final stable syllables have a consonant, an l, and an e at the end of a word. When "l" and "e" are at the end of a word the e is always silent. The schwa (Ə) sound comes before the "l" Pronounced /ull/ like in the word puzzle. It is decoded with a bracket [and is never accented in the final position. When you see the final stable syllable the le brings whatever consonant into its syllable and separates the word. Ex: puz'[zle. Remember when you are analyzing how to decode the words, remember to cover the final stable syllable and then see which one of the decoding rules apply. Refer back to the spelling patterns to practice decoding the words. Please use your knowledge of the skills taught in the book to sound out these words.

If - le syllable is combined with an open syllable, there is no double consonant before the -le. In order words when you hear a long vowel sound in the previous syllable, you usually DO NOT double the consonant. (noble, title, cradle, bugle, candle, jungle).

 If the -le syllable is combined with a closed syllable a double consonant is added before the - le syllable. When the consonant-le endings are followed by a short vowel sound, the first consonant of the ending is usually doubled. (apple, bottle, puddle).

Remember that many final stable syllables have a consonant, an l, and an e at the end. These combinations are called "final" because they are found in the final position of words. They are called "stable" because the pronunciation of each is reliable. Final stable syllables are never accented.

FINAL STABLE SYLLABLE CONSONANT + LE

'[ble	bub'[ble	hum'[ble	fa'[ble	ca'[ble
'[cle	cir'[cle	un'[cle	cy'[cle	popsi'[cle
'[dle	can'[dle	han'[dle	pud'[dle	mid'[dle
'[fle	ruf'[fle	ri'[fle	waf'[fle	snif'[fle
'[gle	jun'[gle	gig'[gle	ea'[gle	trian'[gle
'[kle	twin'[kle	buc'[kle	wrin'[kle	spar'[kle
'[ple	sta'[ple	pur'[ple	sam'[ple	dim'[ple
'[sle	tus'[sle	mea'[sle	has'[sle	ai'[sle
'[tle	bot'[tle	ti'[tle	lit'[tle	tur'[tle
'[zle	puz'[zle	daz'[zle	siz'[zle	driz'[zle

Final Stable Syllable

OTHER FINAL STABLE SYLLABLE ENDINGS

Other Final Stable Syllables word ending include: -sion, tion, ture, cian, tious and cious. The letters ti, si, ci sound like /sh/.

'[tion	elec'[tion	lo'[tion
'[sion	explo'[sion	televi'[sion
'[cian	musi'[cian	physi'[cian

The words ending in (tion, sion, cian) are pronounced sh(Ə)n.

The ending [ture is pronounced /ch(Ə)r/

'[ture	pic'[ture	fix'[ture	fu'[ture

'siŏn   mănsiŏn

'siŏn   tĕlĕvĭsiŏn

'tiŏn   lŏtiŏn

' turĕ   pĭcturĕ

Words ending -cious and tious are normally pronounced /shus/. We have two different ways to spell the /shus/ sound one with a "c" and the other with a "t". There are five letters but only 1 sound which is pronounced /shus/.

'[cious	deli'[cious	spa'[cious
'[tious	cau'[tious	gra'[cious

Consonant Combinations

When you have 2 or 3 letters that make a distinct sound

 ch cheese  ch school

 ch chef

 ck duck

 dge  judge

Special Situations
when it makes a different sound

 ä wä/ch

 bäl/

 banånã

8 ā ā
eigh eight

ge

jŭdge
vc

īgh

līght

gh are "ghost letters", mean
that they're silent and DC
make a sound.

ə
o

ə
love
v cv

y

ŭ   ē
money
vc vv

BREAKDOWN OF EACH VOWEL SOUND

VOWEL SOUND /A/

Long A=13 different ways to make long A			
ei= weigh	eight	sleigh	weight
ay= day	pay	stay	hay	tray
a-e= cake	rake	cage	take	gate
ai= mail	plain	wait	rain	nail
Long a= acorn	aim		basic	apron
ae= maelstrom				
ey= they	hey			
eig= reign				
aigh= straight				
et= ballet				
ea= steak	break			
e= cafe				
Drop y add ies= babies				

Schwa= /uh/	
banana	Canada
camera	about
above	across
a	salad

Short A = /ah/	
map	cat
dad	ham
flat	cab
a can	bat

An A **with one L or two LL's= aw**	
talk	walk
ball	fall

The vowel a before the letter l or after the letters qu or w makes the short /ŏ/ sound and is coded with two dots on top (ä).

VOWEL SOUND /E/

Long E= 8 different ways to make long e

e-e=	concrete	delete	complete	eve	these
ee=	tree	speed	eel	freeze	see
three	seed	cheese	sheep	feet	jeep
ea=	east	heat	bead	least	really
	eagle	easter	team	meal	steal
	leaf	please	earth	sea	eating
ie=	belief	chief	grief	believe	piece
	yield	niece	cookie	shortie	goodie
e=	we	be	she	he	me
	evil	equal	ego	eve	equal

y= (2 or more syllable words = e)

lady	baby	puppy	candy	sunny	windy	dizzy
chilly	every	pretty	worry	Emily	party	family
eld=	field	shield	held	windshield		seldom
	yield	elder	withheld			upheld
ead=	read	bead	head	bedspread		deaf
	cheerleading	dead	bread	lead	ready

Short /e/

Egg	envelope	elephant	elevator	exit	enemy
elk	empty	edge	end	effort	bed
jet	leg	men	net	ten	web
wet	bed	best	help	bet	red

Schwa =/uh/
The
Problem
happen

VOWEL SOUND /I/

Long I= 5 different ways to make long i					
i-e=	time	kite	dime	dice	bike
ie=	pie	tries	tie	diet	tied
igh=	light	knight	bright	night	high
I=	I				
y= 1 syllable words = i					
	fly	dry	by	cry	sky

Short i = /i/						
Iguana	invitation	insect	bib	dig	fin	hit
lid	lip	give	pig	pin	sit	zip

Schwa= /uh/
Family
Emily
University

VOWEL SOUND /O/

Long O= 8 different ways to make long O				
o-e=	nose	bone	globe	cone	hose
oa=	goat	boat	float	soap	coat
ow=	window	grow	know	glow	bow
oe=	toe	foe	doe	goes	Joe
ow=	meadow	window	borrow	bow	snow
ough=	although	dough	bough	enough	cough

O followed by two consonants					
	Go**ld**				
Just letter o					
Oval	hotel	program	total	no	ago

Short O					
dot	box	dog	log	mop	pop
dog	frog	otter	octopus	olive	pot

Schwa /o/
Woman
Police
Television

VOWEL SOUND /U/

Long U=5 different ways to make long U				
u=	unicorn	music	unit	unicycle
	student	uniform	United States	
u-e=	use	cube	rude	mute	cute
	fuse	volume	huge	use	mule
ew=	grew	new	blew	drew	chew
oo=	loose	school	bloom	soon	broom
	moon	spoon	tooth	pool	good
ue=	glue	clue	due	blue	argue
	statue	true	avenue	rescue	value
Long U has 2 sounds - yoo and oo				

Short u = /uh/					
umpire	under	sun	umbrella	cut	rug
tub	cup	hug	gum	bus	supply

PHONO-GRAPHIC WORDS THESE ARE WORDS AND THEIR VOWEL SOUNDS THAT CAN BE USED TO ENHANCE YOUR READING SKILLS. HAVE FUN AND PRACTICE SAYING THEM.

'o-e'

o-e	note
oa	boat
oe	toe
o	most
ow	grow
ough	though
ou	soul
oo	door

'o'

o	pot
au	fraud
aw	lawn
al	walk
a	father
ough	fought
augh	taught

'i-e'

ì-e	kite
ie	cried
i	wild
igh	night
y	fly
eigh	height

'u'

u	tub
ou	touch
o-e	some
a	about

'u-e'

u-e	mule
u	pupil
ew	few
ue	cue

'oo'

oo	boot
ue	blue
ew	new
u	super
ui	suit
u-e	flute
ou	soup
oe	shoe
o	do
ough	through

'a'

| a | cat |

'ow'

ow	cow
ou	out
ough	drought

'i'

| i | in |
| y | myth |

'ee'

ee	meet
ea	seat
ie	chief
y	funny
e	she
i-e	petite
i	variation
ei	re(c)eive
e-e	eve
ey	key

'a-e'

a-e	ape
ai	rain
ay	say
ea	steak
ey	they
eigh	eight
a	paper
ei	vein
aigh	straight

'er'

er	faster
ur	turn
ir	girl
or	work
ear	learn
yr	syrup
ar	dollar

'oy'

| oy | boy |
| oi | soil |

'e'

e	bed
ea	bread
ai	said
ie	friend

'oo'

oo	cook
oul	would
u	put

PHONO-GRAPIX COMPANY IS AN EXCELLENT RESOURCE FOR TEACHERS AND PARENTS.

ABOUT THE AUTHOR

I was born in 1970 in LaCeiba, Honduras and came to the United States at the age of 3. I was raised in Houston, Texas. I graduated from the University of Houston with a B.A. in Education. I am a single mother of a 22-year-old. Twenty-eight years of teaching reading to grades K-2 allowed me to witness the positive impact that my step-by-step phonics instruction had on children's reading and overall literacy. I have put together tips and tricks with targeted practice I learned along the way through my experience. I want children to have a good understanding of why the word is pronounced the way it is by noticing the spelling patterns and decoding strategies within words, not memorizing a word. I was awarded 2023-2024 SHABE Teacher of the Year for the greater Houston area. I feel honored and privileged in receiving this award from my peers. With this in mind, I welcome you to experience a child's reading success as you open this book and begin to apply the targeted, step-by-step reading strategies contained within.

Printed in the USA
CPSIA information can be obtained
at www.ICGtesting.com
LVHW061054200624
783566LV00017B/502